KU-686-151

DK READERS

LEARNING
pre-level 1
TO READ

In the Park

A Dorling Kindersley Book

We like going
to the park.

grass

balls

6

We kick balls
on the grass.

string

bow

kites

We fly kites
in the sky.

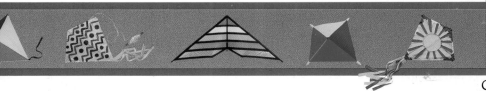

9

bat ————•

We play rounders
with bats
and a ball.

 bats and balls

ball

We watch the ducks
on the pond.

 ducks

pond

feathers

water

We sail boats
on the water.

boats

flag

sail

15

step

climbing frames

16

We go up high on the climbing frame.

slide

 swings

18

We play on the swings.

feet

tyre

seat

head

ear

dogs

20

We run and run
with our dogs.

We ride our bikes
around the park.

 bikes

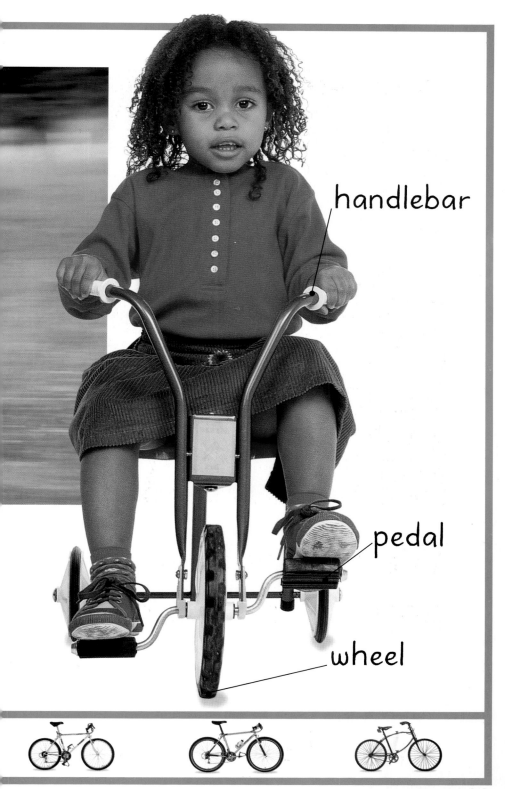

handlebar

pedal

wheel

23

helmet

 skates

We wear our skates to whizz along.

wheel

We play a game
of hide-and-seek.

 hide-and-seek

hand

27

nut

fur

squirrels

28

We watch the squirrels
looking for nuts.

 What do you do

We have lots of fun in the park.

roundabout

n the park?

Picture word list

ball

page 6

kite

page 8

bat and ball

page 10

duck

page 12

boat

page 14

climbing frame

page 16

swing

page 18

dog

page 20

bike

page 22

skate

page 24

hide-and-seek

page 26

squirrel

page 28